BLOSSOMS OF BEING

"Glimpses from the Beyond"

Prof. Manju Bala

Preface

When I behold the wonderful creation around me, I get transported to the world beyond the physical. I find the tumult in my mind has calmed. I find myself internally ignited to give shape to what I feel in normal life. My hand is inundated with inexplicable joy. There is an inner compulsion to write down what I feel quite often, the metaphysical issues of life do arouse my attention. But then comes a moment when I wish to ask new questions from inside me. When I seek answers and find none available, I get attuned to the universe around me. In that state of mental dissolution, in that unified moment, inspiration from the blue unites my heart, and I feel like capturing the moment and writing down what comes to me in all spontaneity.

So, all my poems are outpourings of such moments when I cease to be a separate individual and when I become one with the seen and the unseen world.I hope the readers will have a taste of the sense of wonder I feel watching the world around me and when my mind dissolves into the eternal world.

Contents

1

In Love with Life

Passionately in love with
This beautiful mystery
Which can wreck and break
And make one freak

Yet beautifully mesmerizing
A beautiful track it is
Full of scenic beauty
And horrific death routes

It is in itself complete
Mixture of varied tastes
To taste a bit
None of them is a waste

Unplanned, we embarked
 On this path
Not even knowing when
Got to go past

Sometimes it passes through
Beautiful pastures, jungles, and mountains
And others, it goes through deserts and oceans
Many a times so fast, almost breathtaking
Others, it comes to a halt all of a sudden

The rollercoaster ride
Or enjoying the sight
The fear the pain
Nothing to lose or gain

Just to experience
The journey we are put on
Can't step out of it
Have to be within

Tasting all the buffet
With tears, fears, and smiles
Lack, happiness, and abundance
Totally in and observing from outside

Accumulating experiences, things, people
Memories, pleasures, and pain
Stocking everything carefully
Leaving behind one day with no gain

Yet this profound experience
In itself, it is transforming
Despite the bad stuff
The beauty is charming

One day, when one outgrows
These momentary shifts of journey
He can admire the profundity
Of this experience so transforming

Given what may
One can't fail to say
Despite all the struggle and strife
One is in love with life

Colour Combination

Blue is the sky
With white clouds
Wandering quite high

White has turned the earth
With pure snow, it is worth

Green are trees
On the hill tops
Snow as water
From top does drop

Colourful are the people
Walking on the road

Darkens the hilltop
The shadow does come
Clouds race in sky
To block the sun

Birds do chirp
Hop and jump
Cows do stand
Soaking in the sun

Here goes the horn
The bus does come
To catch it in time
People do run

Bare apple trees
They do dance
With blowing wind
Don't let go the chance

Stray dogs pee on the pole

Walk through the snow

Quite far they have to go

Marking the boundaries is their goal

Run

Sunday, Monday, or Friday

Each morning, each day

Get up early and switch off the alarm,

Drink a glass of warm water

Brush your teeth, get fresh

Tie the laces, get dressed

Hit the track when it's still dark

Follow your route, make your mark

Get into rhythm; fix yourself

Listen to the music of footsteps

Sway to and fro
Glide head to toe
Get into the natural beat
Let it on its own increase

Feel the majestic balance
Relish the dance between steps
The jump of one foot in the air
The landing of the other so fair

The beauty of the movement
The rhythm of breathing
A march forward
Be it plain, uphill, or downhill

Talk to air
Cut the rain
Sweat in sun
In snow do win

Move ahead always
Reach for the target
With a mind quite clear
A heart full of vigour

Complete the run
With a sense of fulfilment
And feeling of fun
Achievement becomes a habit

Strength, valour, and goal achieving
Become the innate qualities
The mind is all peaceful,
The heart placid
A deep sense of accomplishment
Physical, mental, emotional, and spiritual

Sitting Outside

Wind is blowing

Teasing the hair

A cold shiver is felt

In the month of June

Trees dancing, river flowing

This endless music is blowing

The place is profuse with

Tweets of birds, visible and unseen

A buttercup is dancing

Shaken tipsy turvy from stem

It enjoys the rhyme and play

Be whatever, whichever it may

A tiny black butterfly

Flutters all around

Is unmindful of wind

And neither is it bound

Engulfed in the tree

By the wind blowing over

Branches, twigs, and leaves

Awakened from stupor

This sustained motion

In objects of nature

Like wind and water

Is contrasted well by the rocks and Earth

5

Meera

White teeth curl on forehead
Lively eyes shining bright
Uneven whites covered by lips
With a tap of lipstick on them

That suit of yours
Green and golden mixed
Ever brimming smile
Did the talking by itself

You talked more with
Eyes, smiles, gestures, and fidgeting
Innocently clicking tongue
The way you felt shy

The moment you entered the door
Shy and hesitant
Then, mustering courage,
Called me and ran away laughing

The laughter was imminent
The smile perpetual
On the slightest issue
You walked to me

With hopeful eyes
And loving command
You insisted that I do
Solve your problem

People were around
Working, but it gave you
Assurance when I did
Things for you

I do appreciate you

For the trust you

Invested into me

The love we shared

The relationship is full of

Respect, care, love, admiration

You a super girl

What a runner you were!

The dance, especially the Ghoomar

You were always outstanding

I, your proud teacher

You all were my pride

My concerned, strangely obedient student

My face lit up the moment I saw you

With heartfelt best wishes

I just wished day and night

The best life could offer,

To loving, simple, sober, talented

Students like you

We did resonate on
The high level of love,
Purest form, just trying to give
Only care and acceptance

The farewell party
You all were shining
Brimming with beauty
In your best form

The happiest moments
We all danced together
The day was yours
Your happiness was echoing
Within my heart

With all wishes for
Your brightest future
We departed formally
Here's to your promising tomorrow

The day was the heaviest one
It told its toll inside
Benumbed with heaviness
The unescapable was the accident

Already, I could feel

Deep down in spine

The strange silence was glaring

Staring into my eyes,

The sighs, the heaviness of breath

The news was devastating

Could not understand

What was it

Could not have already happened

Yes, I wanted to rush

To your side for a last meeting

I went, reached out

But your body was already

On the pyre consumed in those

Flames, I do remember

I do feel strange

Gripping grief, I still remember

I do remember your smile

That kept flashing

Each second in the mind

I could not console
Your bereaved father
In tears, I wanted to
Tell him, "No, don't weep! "
For a brave girl

And wanted to tell
The grief is not his only
I too lost you, you
Are also closest to my heart,
I too loved you the way
He did

Dear Meera, life has
Started again, slowly,
We started the normal routines
Started enjoying, but dear,
When I see other students

I am reminded of you
I love you and ever after
Witnessing you leave forever
Can't believe it has happened

Miss you dear MEERA

In heart, you are here

Alive forever, dear Meera

6

Childhood Recollections

Children love fun
To hop and to run
So was I
Who loved to play

Studying in 6th standard
Rains were the reminder
Time for fun, to laugh, and run
Is nearing and is about to come

Those long-awaited staycations
Used to come as a great relief
Though the time was of months
For us children, it was too brief

We ran from field to field in pouring rain
Elders tried to stop, but in vain
Like birds, we flew from tree to tree
Hopping, jumping, we were totally free

The whole earth was only ours
The blowing wind the shining sun
Bathing from morning till evening
In the incessant monsoon rain

Danced to the music of thunder and lightning
Leapt on water, splashed it with feet
We held one another's hands
Our train didn't stop until dark

With hearts filled with a full day's thunder
It didn't take much for us to slumber
After the whole day of fun and play,
With an excited effort to wake up early,
For another day to thrive and sway

Sleeping Unmindful

Beautiful eyes are fully closed
The glowing face at rest
The breath-following rhythm
Dances to its own beat

Thy lips are glowing
The face is fully reposed
Thy beauty has thus been enhanced
As if you are in a trance

The brows are a little displaced
The posture a little distracted
The stiffness, elegance is absent
Cute innocence is prevalent

In deep sleep, you are
Far from the ordinary world
All pretension and attempts
And activities are at a halt

This sleep has a spell
What made you dwell
In a divine-like world
Possessing flawless charm
In sphere, still and calm

8

Take Heart

Until when will we be

Just watching and planning

Postponing to live

So, let's come have watch

And planned enough

Let us start living

To what extent are we

Going to doubt our capabilities,

Judging and seeing

Ourselves from others' angles

Always trying to find

What is lacking in us?

Why not we embrace ourselves?

In our full entirety

And appreciate the things

Which makes us 'US'

Being thankful to them

On blessings, let us focus

Until when will we ponder?

Others to be perfect and wonderful,

Only their lives are proper

Ours are just gross

That we are the only

Underprivileged

We need not be like others

We might lack things like them

But dear friend

We have ourselves

We just have us

So why not relish

Our very existence

We are here in our entirety
Not planning any more
Not skimming on possibilities
But diving straight into
Things we have to do

The ones we want to do
Or somewhere in a corner
And depths of our heart
We always aspired to do

But due to some fear
Doubt, insecurities
Or to some misgivings,
We chose to sit by
And kept postponing

So why not just right now
Dive deep into that
And scale all the heights
And later on, realise

O really I had such

A great potential having done that,

So, let's dive into living

Right now, right here

9

Loving Myself

Falling in love with myself,
Slowly and steadily

Almost having spent half of my life
I have just come to realise
The most amazing being
Of course, it has been me

My beauty I hardly
Took time to appreciate
Though I looked at the mirror
Every day searching for the tiniest flaws

Charming face, lovely lips

A beautiful body full of grace

I bet everyone glanced

How did I miss the chance?

After doing so much, as such

After having as much as I hold

How I just simply skipped

Such beauty as gold

I cared for things and people

I cared so much more

At the cost of my being

All that does nothing bring

I subjected myself to things

Which don't deserve me

How did I love others?

On the cost of real me

If I don't love myself,

Passionately enough to hold

How can I love others?

In their true essence

I might have projected onto
Others the way I wanted,
Assigning them a special place
By letting me down, the space

Now, when I am falling
In love with myself
I do realise the way
I deprived myself of the same

In order to be lovable,
I strived to change myself
Each time being more insecure
I added to inner insecurities

I took others' judgment
Without filter each time
I assumed myself a worthless creature,
And then started to whine

The opinion of those
Who themselves are confused,
The fearful people
And the dangerous ones

I left myself alone
Whenever I needed myself the most
I felt miserable whenever
I became a victim of mistreatment

People did wrong
I punished myself
Always thinking
Fault may lie in me

And now I know
I was right
The fault lay in me,
I was the guilty one

It was a choice that I made
To believe in all stupidity
I gave permission
To be treated like that

I was the one
Who was selfish
Wanted people to stay
The ones who underestimated me

The one who would settle for anything
Just want to assume things
Everything is good, all is well
I am happy, life is meaningful

Now I know that was a trap
There were no boundaries, no roadmap
I was toying with everything
Self-fulfilling prophecies and self-generated woes

Was this a simple thing?
So complicated to understand
It is I who matters,
Then comes the other one

I needed to love myself too much
To be affected by others' truths
To be all love and just love
Be the bases of all my actions

Not the prejudices, the set patterns
Nor the needs and insecurities
Just pure love, only love
For me and for all

That River

Rubbing her eyes

She woke up

Seeing the world around

Was she much amazed

Enjoyed the surroundings

Was filled with intoxication

New experience, filled with sensation

Was the whole existence

But still, she was stiff
Confined in an environment
To be suffocated to death
In the surrounding mud

Deep had she to think
What should she do
To get smothered slowly
Or to start for the unknown

Fate, which does exist
Or not is a mystery
Whether she will be wiped out
Or will she create history?

She tried hard
To live in the mud
But no use was it
She was dying and drying

Had she to move
To be alive and agile,
So was the only way
She was now confined

What to do, where to go?

She was quite weak and slow,

She had to flow and flow,

Didn't she know how to grow

Each straw, each blade of grass

Stopped her with full force

Each pebble the utmost hindrance

Did it cause

The grass and weed

What to talk of plants and trees?

Every small to big thing,

Was just an obstruction

She fought fiercely

To build her way a bit

She had to live and die,

Each day, striving hard

Slowly, her vigour started

Showing her undying will

The mud, the weed, the pebbles

Started exerting more power

Now the river decided
Firmly to move forward,
Unmindful of all obstructions
Over them, around them, she flowed

Very slowly, step by step
She gained speed unnoticed
But the journey was
Already set in

She gained momentum
Started sliding on the grass
The pebbles, the plants
The flow started getting speed

Its existence was established
It had taken shape
The initial obstructions
Were now the things of the past

She became large
In volume and size
Now its own completeness
Did she realise

She moved, dragged, crushed

Whatsoever came its way

Was fierce by now

Uprooted everything in its way

She roared and thundered

Cutting the edges

Grinding the rocks

Breaking all the blocks

It became deeply fierce

Dangerous and scary

The struggle for survival

Resulted in an authoritative revival

It leapt and swelled

And from heights

With dignity, it fell

With all vigour, energy prevailed

Slowly the struggle started subsiding

The aggressive river has now

Started moving with grace

The fierceness replaced by elegance

It reached the plains where
The whole area was for it only
She was all free, boundless
She started calming down

Thus, the river let go
All the past struggles
To high elegance
Her gait became graceful

It is shining
With the grace of struggle
The wisdom of ages
Of life of a river and its stages

She keeps smiling
Soothing the world around
Giving and enjoying
It rejoices in its own existence

Secretly, it knows it was 'right'
When it decided to flow,
To march forward to an unknown fate
To memorably gleam and glow

Cute Face

Cute face, full of grace

Lovely smile, healthy vibes

Spreading joy, O little boy,

Sometimes bold, sometimes coy

Let us play, you and I,

Some new games today we will try

O playful being, don't feel shy

Enjoy

Flower do bloom

Stars do shine

Birds do chirp

Colourful butterflies do fly

Let's go to the meadows

To see the blooming flowers

Dancing in the wind

Strikingly fresh as if after the shower

In the ocean of my heart
You can go deep and far
Fathom the depth at large
Come out safe and enlarged

Try not to play it safe
Struggle not to be brave
Float, drift, and just sway
Only then will you find a way

Enjoy the sensation
Of the great fall
Before hitting the bottom
Glide in far and at large

Gently will you
Touch the bottom
You will find every support,
Will be pushed upside again
Just easy, you have to remain

The love in heart will hold you tight,
Will let you come up safe
Will lift you gently
Feel the warmth of love before you take flight

Spirits may remain high

Or maybe sometimes low

Doesn't stop anywhere

Time just flows

So go on, enjoy yourself

Either in the core of the heart

Or be by yourself

Just enjoy this beautiful life

13

How Does the Morning Come?

How does the morning come?

As our eyes do open

One more day added

So starts the new one

So many dreams

And different resolutions

Does today differ?

From yesterday

Let us come out
From the walls of the head
Thinking, repeating, analysing
The pieces of memory

On an hourly, minutely basis
And see the things around
With new curiosity
As if seen for the first time

Let the curtains fall apart
Close your eyes and be calm
Leave the worry of the world
Let us go deep inside

Thoughts will come; let them
Don't struggle to fight them
Just observe what is going on
Inquisitiveness is to play its part

These few minutes you just
Spend time observing yourself
Marvellous is the thought who
Is this what is thinking?

Just enjoy the flow

In your body

The sensations, tingling

Let the thought come and go

Now you are someone

Watching yourself

From far observing

Everything is going on in the moment

14

Let's Go, You and I

When clouds are not in the sky
Come and stroll for a while
Open your heart with a smile

So cheerful is everything
Trees are enjoying the dance
Are brimming with life
To see it all is a great chance

The sunlight is scattered
All over equally
But the effect brings out
All differences are uniquely

The river has started to glow

The green trees became lighter

Rocks seem more manifest

Tarnished has become the white snow

15

Dig a Little Deep

Things are bright
And very light
On the surface
Beautiful face

A little deep
Though quite steep
If have to move
Things are to be removed

Work under progress
Thus, going through the process
Distinguishing and identifying
Analysing and categorising

Is constantly going on
Seeing judging
Automatic reactions and responses
Are forming constantly

A little further
If move we
Is a place
For us to see

Like a black hole
The place not known
Is such strange
Can't be understood

The little further
Surface starts getting hard
A place so reclusive to us
We don't let anything pass

Inside, there is a throbbing

Life in its innocence

So tender, so fragile

Here lies our whole essence

Once in life

We were all like that

Slowly, it became clear

We need to protect that

We hardened outer sphere

Every time things touched life

Shook it shocked it

Furthermore, the outer hardened

The little life we have

The more innocence in it

So much love and vulnerability,

We fight hard to protect

As deep down, we know

This is the thing that matters

Is this the only way
To deal with it
Or can we open
All the locks

Let flow the essence
In full swing like a flood
Break all boundaries
With a strong force of love

Shatter all the chairs
Break all boundaries
Make life the ruling guide
Let love take its course
Let love be the only guiding force

16

Snow Flakes

Flakes gliding from the sky
In grand majesty
To see them coming
Down is a privilege

They do descend
With full glory
One by one
Sky appears flowery,

To stand and see

The beautiful flakes

Descending from sky

Is transcending in itself

Like we are standing

In the space

Somewhere in cosmos

Watching the thing revolving

Everything is in motion,

Seeming spiralling

A movement so profound,

Like a shower of cosmic substance

Like the asteroid belt,

Between Mars and Jupiter

Spiralling, moving fast,

The sight is majestic as long as it lasts

17

The Sun is Burning

In the sky
Clouds are there
But not so high,

The white sheet
Spread on ground
Trees, twigs, and roofs,
Started depleting

From white to transparent
To water flow
Shining separately, each atom
With blinding glow,

Has started falling
From the trees
As if snow is bound
To something on the ground

Visible are patches
Of earth from snow
Turning into water
Does it flow

The sound of water
Dripping from roofs
Has filled the place
With music so unique,

Tit bits of clouds
In sky far and wide
Have set again for
Their further ride

This humble abode
Of beautiful glow
Is a gift to humanity,
To see nature in full majesty

The Innocence is Prevalent

Innocence is prevalent,

So is cruelty

Life is nourishing,

So is it faulty

Where to focus

The choice is ours

Success seems fulfilling,

Failure feels hard

Disheartening and obstructing,

Or does it take us ahead

What to make of

The choice is ours

Innocent Snow

The Snow Doesn't Know

In all white purity
It is untouched
What does it imply
For humanity at large

Too innocent it is,
How much discomfort
It causes
The snow doesn't know

The Way it Be

Let the wind blow

And the sun glow

The birds enjoy flight,

The day is to be much bright

The clock to tick

The day to grow to its peak

Time to go by

Changes to be high

People to talk

Give anyone shock

Let everyone be idle,

Let everything be brittle,

Just let things be as they are

No Movement

Only peace
The one which is intense,
Is all prevalent

The one that is complete
Despite its only existence
Which is far from the physical world
Though it does offer
Anything worthwhile for survival

So deep is this peace
That it has engulfed
Anything and everything
The whole universe
Into itself thoroughly

All sounds, all distractions
All the noise and din
Even the thoughts
Coming and going emotions

Are nothing being soaked
Into this peace
Despite being there
Is hardly noticeable

It is the peace
Which is strong
Which is alive
And the dominant one

The rivulet that flows
Freely and vigorously
It moves continuously,
Day and night

So, fills the forest

With a sweet rhyme

Sometimes the blowing wind,

Adds to the colourful rhyme of it

For the centuries

Has it existed

Till the times to come

Will it be here

Making the woods come alive

Letting the vegetation thrive,

Other things may give way

But it will always survive

22

I am Not

I am not knowledgeable
That which is transforming,
I am not just the body
As it seems, I have got more

I am not the deadening sadness
Nor the ecstatic laughter
Nor am I the extreme of compassion
Or the venomous hatred

Not the anguished tear
Neither the frightening fear
Nor the repelling stranger
Not the sobbing close one

The thoughts that occupy
No, I am none of them
The feelings and emotions that trigger
I am none of their figure

I am affected by all these things
All these are reflected in my being
I am the ground for them to play games
Yet they don't change me; I remain the same

A vessel as natural
As things may seem
Or even more simple
Which never may be seen

23

Play the Game

Play the game

To the fullest

Live each second

Till it lasts

Regarding things

Others than yourself

As the more important

Has become the norm

That talent of someone
Or the impressive skill
Excite us enough
To strengthen the belief

All the things
Bright and beautiful
Distinct and superior
Whatever we can observe

Are the ones that one can master
Do as much as you can
Or at least willingly want
What you wish to do and be

Be whatever you have to,
Do whatever you like to,
Break your own rules
Challenge self-imposed boundaries

Break your zone
Behave differently
Be little eccentric
Or be a nerd

Achieve unimaginable

Be unstoppable

Toil little hard

Transform entirely

Let the judgments go dizzy

And the critics go crazy

Let your mentors be perturbed

Let well-wishers be disturbed

As you will do something

Beyond your labelled capabilities

It will shake and shock

The lake of belief into ripples

Let those ripples become ocean currents

Let them play havoc

Let the tsunami come

Wash away everything prior to that

Everything will be new

You have the power

To bring in novelty

Just trust thyself wholeheartedly

Accept yourself immensely

Love more deeply

Only you matter

As the only one

This game is yours

You are the hero

It's your test

The winning is yours

The game, the world

Lasts for you

Till you are here

Do play to the fullest

As the moment

You will leave

The game will cease

For you are gone

The world may not end

The things will be there

The only difference, you

You will be no more

Your world would end the moment you are gone

24

Sunlight

Dear sunlight
You are the only bright
Only you have the power
To bring all objects to light

The dullness of all objects
Gives way the moment
You smile and spread delight
Beautiful and bright

The flowing water
Becomes pearls like
Crystal clear with
A shine to fullest

The green fields
Trees and forests
Were beautiful earlier
And attractive enough

But the moment
You shine it comes
To live with a glow
That constantly grows

Smile the trees
Dances the branches
With a new texture
Are lost in immense joy

25

This Very Moment

The murmuring noise of river aside
The wind playing with open hair
The chirping of birds all around
The life brimming in all sounds

Let's take a little nature walk
To the tree today, we will talk
Fill ourselves with nature deeply
Entire nature is beautiful and green

The butterfly was fluttering around chair
Birds tweet and chirp everywhere
Clouds spread a white sheet on the sky
Running a race on the blue so high

The children can be heard playing
The tinkering sound from afar
The noise and din of daily life
All life forms thus struggle and strive

Everything is manifest, strikingly agile
In its fullness, in a while
The tiny representation of a complete process
The whole universe in this very instant

26

Jamun Tree

Sturdy stem breaching branches
Fully grown was that Jamun tree

All covered with green leaves
Blackened by the ripening Jamun
Weighing down fruit-laden branches
There it stood in full majesty

Children loved the yielding ones
Which swayed as if to welcome
Running, we went to the tree
Which gave bags of fruit absolutely free

Feet emerged in mud as we did climb
Very easy was our triumph
From branches to twigs did we roam
The tree was our second home

Since the time when fruits started ripening
To the time when the season comes to an end
That tree was our daily companion,
On it, our days were spent

We spent the hot afternoons,
Under the shade of its branches
The pouring evening with heavy rain,
We left the tree with a gust of refrain

As time approached to go home,
We didn't want to leave it alone
With a sad heart and heavy steps
With utmost unwillingness, we crept

One Smile

One smile can change,
The world around
Can lit up the fire
Provide the human warmth

One smile can travel,
The world around
Passing from one person to another,
Moving on further and further

Yeah, it is contagious

Spreads all over

You start the one

Smiley, the whole world will turn

The most innocent and cute,

Is the one that comes from the heart

The very moment it beholds someone

A smile is something that all enjoy

It lightens up the hearts,

Of those who give and receive

It is the purest form of joy

A smile is something that all enjoy

So why should we be deprived?

A fountain of joy thus provided,

Why not take a sip and take a dip?

In the ocean of happiness so deep

28

Imparting Education

While imparting education,
Comes to mind a question
Are the problems being sorted?
Or the vision is being distorted

Knowledge, education, or information
Where is the real transformation?
Something new we are to create
Or old values are being cracked

Struggling half of our lives

Toiling very hard

Preparing for a future

Which seems quite far

A life in preparation

In memorizing of the already existent

Which type of enlightenment?

What type of existence?

Research is a must

Whether old or rut

Degrees have predominance

What a coincidence

Learning something that is

The farthest from life

So artificial, so monotonous

With the ever-new methods to learn

To learn to cram to memorise
And then to use it
Work hard day and night
Prepare for a future assumedly bright

But how many people can
Just hold with lifeless rut
Already half-done generation
Is preparing a generation to rust

Who will be their progeny?
With sullen faces and fake smiles
With artificial gentlemanly affectation
Will be lifeless and devoid of affection

A race of zombies
Do we want to create?
No life, no laughter
Can we mend, or are we late?

With all our deep concern
Of a better future for our descendants
Are we sure they are safe?
Or are we leading them to the cliff?

Like our lives struggled halfway

Are we going to inflict theirs?

With postponement until they reach

Some decent place where they can

Bargain for a living, at least,

If they could ever make it up to that

29

The Inner Bitch

Sometimes when things
Are going all well
There is something inside
Which is hurting to the hell

Call it ego
Or immaturity may be stupidity
But something gets triggered
A deep-down message, it figures

All this happens
In an instance
To stop it or escape it
There is no chance

A flood comes
And takes everything along,
The knowledge, the wisdom
The sense of judgement is gone

In the heat of the moment
Everything becomes heated,
The vision, the reason
All mental faculties are distorted

Very slowly does
The cooling process start
When the head is done
Then the heart starts

Why did all that need to happen?
Couldn't we resist and stop that?
Where all tenderness had gone
Why even that madness was on

A repenting heart

An overwhelmed one

Contemplating over

What inner bitch has done

30

What We Want

Throughout life, goes the process
Of learning and earning
Very curious are we to find out,
What all things do we desire?

In different ages and stages
Of life, we pursue goals
Which makes sense for that time
And need not to be analysed

Kind of all time
We are making an assessment
And setting desires as to
What all we want

Picking from friends
From our social circle
And from books, we read
From idealized persons or styles

And list out things
That we want to have,
To do to attain

If influences are taken away
Will be musing as to
What is it that I want?
What if my heart is
Running behind all impressions

If reactions and triggers
Will be taken away
One will be left bereft of everything,
To contemplate what he wants

31

Sunday Morning

Beautiful morning

Full of sounds

Twits of birds

Vehicles passing by,

Clouds overhead

Wet is the ground

Smiling trees

Playing with wind

Hidden is the sun

On its very day

Yes, it's a Happy Sunday

No Meaning

This is a consistent flux,
Jingling of mixed flavours,
A flow full all the time
Be mindful or forget; it's your choice

Circulate as many theories
Or philosophies as much as you want
Justify whatever you can
Do however you want

It's not even the speck of flux
Neither does this flux care
For any amount of change
Or turning the world upside down

Millions of books may be propounded
Beaming with countless explanations
One may figure out the cosmos
Hardly, it matters anyway

All the melodies, the jarring noises
Are one and the same
The nonchalant doership and inertia
Come from the same place

The thinking tanks, the emotional tornadoes
Fatiguing activities day and night
The most rapid change or the primitive silence
Ultimately, you are the one thing

The din and silence are the same
Success and failure are one
Life and death are identical
The choice and imposition are alike

Duality and non-duality
Has nothing to do with reality
Every reality is individual and different
No parameter to measure what is what

Nothing is more or less
Nothing is good or bad
Nothing is true or false
No labelling, no meaning

No, teaching the flux just is
Neither was nor will be
Just is on and on

33

Enslaved

I find here myself
Wriggling in the abyss,
No top no bottom
A kind of messed-up space

Life is a very simple phenomenon,
Everything is the way it is
All the suffering is the result,
Of one's attitude and actions

How can one just think
Unfair is the deal
Spreading hatred and jealousy
And expecting to be loved

This separateness has just doomed,
How lovingly vices have bloomed,
One's own vices robs him
Of all, love, peace, and joy

It's none other than the one
Who has brought himself to this end?
Where one finds the wounded essence
Every touch seems so brittle

Every touchy ego finds
All the things can be a challenge,
So sticky gets in everyone's way
Bringing in misery time and again

Blaming the world around
But the culprit lies within
The inner hatred is projected,
To the things different from oneself

Jealousy, the projection of inner evil,
Justified through all blame game
Belittling others can satisfy how?
When the little one is inside,

Anger projected at people
As they seem to crush the soul,
But when looked deep down
It's one's greed that has

Enslaved, entangled, and attached
To everything that everything seems bad
But its mine, me
I enslaved myself

34

The World of Ants

Quite busy, walks dizzy

Fast still zig-ziggety

Checking for smell

Searching all the way so well

So busy are they

Going the whole way

Wherever the sight goes

Ants are there more and more

These tiny creatures
Yet intricately crafted,
As tiny they are
So are they fast

Their six legs
Make them superfast
The intellect and senses
Make them smarter

Effortless they are
In their interaction
With whatever comes their way,
Keep on walking, they don't stay

Is there any place
Where they are not
On rocks, plants, soil, trees
Be it road, home, or concrete

Are they omnipresent?
Everywhere they are present
Out of nowhere, they do come
As if they are nearby always

They live on the same planet as we do
Work hard like us, they do too,
Beautifully organised homes, they too have
Very much like us, they are

Or maybe they are
Agile, active, and light
Always set for flight
Working day and night

So engrossed they are,
In whatever they do
It seems they just love
Or live for what they do

Not very much like us
And so much more like us,
Is the beautiful and complete,
The world of ants

35

The Cute Bee

The cute bee, so are thee,
Again, hovering around
These purple flowers,
Bushes and the tree

Sure, you can't stay away,
From the nectar they give
Hopping from one flower to another
You are looking for the better ones

And why not, you are the queen
You are the solitary bee
The whole bush belongs to you
Do enjoy the way you feel to

Not only this, there are many more,
Yellow, white or so
All the flowers there are for you,
Take as much nectar as you like

O you have got other friends as well?
So, you all are having a great time
So happy to see you enjoy
Thanks for the unique joy

You have given this joy by your
Earthly activities so charming,
It's beautiful to see you fly
So leisurely sucking the essence of a flower

Bless you, bless your ways
Be here, yes, you may
Swing like this and do stay,
Immense love for you all the way

36

2020

In the first quarter,
In March, the panic started spreading

A virus noble one,
Has started taking a toll
In Wuhan city, China
But discussions spread throughout the whole world

Country got locked down
People confined to their homes
Chaos, apprehension, and fear
It seemed as though something strange had happened

"Unprecedented" was all this
People in the dark
Not knowing what it's all about
The situation is quite stark

People are struck all over the places
In different countries and states
All of a sudden, all activities stopped,
No one knew what to hope

37

Incorrigibly Romantic

It started in early childhood

Had a feeling of being damn special

Imagined myself to be the most coveted princess,

To be loved more than anything

A dreamer far off from

The actual world of reality

But special, gifted, or wanted

Felt myself to be the one

All life's trials and turbulences
And the knowledge and facts
Yes, they do hide very well
But could not erase that special world

The world where I am the Princess
The whole love is pouring towards me
I am the saviour of humanity
Everything rests on my will

The world where I can
Go wherever one feels like going
Far from the mundane world of reality
My own abode of ever-pouring love

This world, this kingdom
Is mine only where I mattered
Even the earth-shaking life
Could not move a bit of it

It is complete and intact
Whenever I rid of the world around
I can leap in this dreamy land
With myself, the happiest ever I can spend

How all conditioning,

Worldly knowledge and information

Could never touch

That dreamy, romantic world inside

Which is safe so deep in the ocean of heart

38

Letting the Shields Down

As of right now, I am letting the shields
Of shoulds, coulds, woulds down,
Feeling more at ease,
And in total peace

It's a feeling of being back home
As if picking the one I left way back
A piece of me or the real me, which was
Buried under the lists of shoulds

I was never ever at peace with myself,
Putting on so many masks
Denying the real face of me,
In the process of denial

The anger, the bitterness, the pettiness
The jealousy, the hatred, the stupidity,
Was to be replaced with
The nicety, the loving, the caring
Being timid was shown as daring

I just acted so well,
Wiped every bit of originality,
From the memory of every cell
Showed the face that sells

But how long can one fool?
Don't ask, sure very long
But the bursts of anger and madness
Will come to the front now and then

Which will tell the level of pain
The drama is all in vain
Neither you nor anyone else
Has there anything to gain

The world needs not to be fooled
The biggest loss, do you know?
Is the loss of your very self,
While you search which mask you really are

Still, you can't make sense,
You have lost so intense
Till one day, by chance
You reach a place

Still trying to figure out,
How to fix, looking for tricks
Titbit that might work
Then at last, it may occur

Put down all the masks
Let down the shield
There is no enemy
You are fighting just yourself

Whatsoever we are told to change,
Are the real we
One thing that needs to be done,
Is to be real WE

To not just accept
The angry and hateful me
But to love it all the way
Whatsoever is the real me

Putting down the guards
And being the way you are,
Owning all of it in its entirety
Is the way to final peace

Nothing is there to prove,
We are already complete
Just loving and being
That's what all it means

We are already lovable and worthy
Need not change anything
First, make peace within yourself
Rest, everything will fall into place

The child you are was abandoned
And was told it was not good enough
You know, just hold his hand,
Just love him and tell him, 'He is the best'

39

If I Die Today

The world will be the way it was,

Very few eyes may be wet

Nothing else will change

Only this me will be wiped

A body and a mind

Which finds itself struggling

In conflicts and strife

Searching for inner peace

All the transactions in the
Name of love and hate will stop,
People will be living and thriving
Even after I am gone

When I am alive
Wanna do things
How can I just take pressure
That suddenly will cease

For people who don't even care
I am losing sense of me
The ones who deny my existence
Even when I am alive

40

Midst Confusion

Why are you wondering, dear?
Have you got some fear?
It's all right to be in
Situations like this,

When nothing makes sense
It seems strange dance,
Which time is doing right now
Of course, you can't figure out where and how

When the mind can't grasp

What is going on

Trying to reach conclusions

Just leads to confusion

It's alright to be

Drift and scattered being

When nothing seems to be working out

Let us say just 'Wow'

Life has its ways to show

Same track, it will not go

One will stumble and fall

When he least expects it all

But the reaction that it cause

Should go some way it was not supposed,

Before getting into the reaction

Why not just take a pause?

The situation is just as it is

Nothing right, nothing wrong

Yes, the mind is trying to cling to

Anything, whatever it can find

To come to a conclusion
To things as dark or light
Based on previous patterns
Making them stronger for further future use

We do understand, dear mind,
You want to draw a picture of
The things that are happening
Some conclusions to pass judgement on

But can you stop and let go?
The need to make sense of anything
Yes, it's a very scary place to be in
Let's be a little brave, not trying to fit in

Here, there, or anywhere
Let's not point out in black and white,
Let's not fight about wrong or right
It seems to be a useless strife

As whatever happened is over,
Let's not play it on and on
It is just the way it was,
Nothing's gonna change it a bit

So, let's fully accept
That nothing makes sense,
Let it fully settle down
In the complete presence

And see in full clarity
That a thing has already happened,
Accepting it the way it happened
Can decide what to do next

How Long on this Planet?

I don't know for how long

I will stay on this planet

In this body, here where

I feel like I will go on forever

Hair started to grey

But childhood does stay

Years rolled away

As if everything was this way

Everything changes
But there is some feeling,
That doesn't change
A surety to exist

Taking life for granted
Not feeling the need to admire,
Whatsoever life offered with love
Kind of went on finding faults

Not only things and people
But with my own self, the most
Kept seeing or trained to see
My unique things as bad ones

This duality of inside manifested
Outside and saw everywhere
Only what might not work
And what is wrong with anything

So bleak and negative became
The attitude and misery became a habit
Neither loving nor admiring,
Either me or anyone else,

Failed to admire a beautiful body
Failed to see this brilliant mind,
Remembered only the struggle
Diminished the successes of life

Life gives every experience
Which one could possibly have
Now choosing to admire the immensity,
Open to feel it in its entirety

42

Fighting the Beggars

You, you give me assurance,

Of being there for me

You give importance

And all the attention you have got

You came with all sweetness

Promises of all love and care

I am going to be your back

And you are my preference

Thus started thing
Call it anything
Initial phase love and praise
Slowly ceasing to put in much effort

The story is known
So long story short
Nobody wants to give in
Nor does anyone falter

So the people just walk away
Expecting each other to give,
What they want, not willing to give,
What others expect of them

Thus are fighting
The beggers with each other,
To give them what they want
Which both may be lacking or unwilling,
In the first place, to possess

43

Shambhavi

I have got a gift
The gift is life unwrapping
All the time it's within me
Every day it is flourishing

The gift is so unique
One could never imagine,
Such a beautiful thing
Has ever existed

Every day it increases
Within me it grows
The life is lighter
The joy is greater

The things which bothered me more
Are not that much bothersome anymore
The fears which gripped so strongly,
Seemed to have been blown

The worries, the tensions
Are no more to be mentioned
Things are there
But the meanings have dropping

Life has found a flow
It glides to and fro
Less friction, fewer restrictions
Binding things it doesn't know

Thanks for such a gift
Oh! Dear master of mine
The gift is life-giving
And it is divine

Here Right Now

I am here right now
In this very moment
Present to all possibilities
Open to all probabilities

Here am I
In this very moment
Fully awake and attentive,
To everything all around

I am listening to talks
I am registering the giggles
The sound of a flowing river
The chirping of the birds

To the amalgamation of
Various voices and sounds
To all kinds of
Available sights,

To the various sensations
Within my body
To the coming going
Breath I am witness

The heartbeat
The watch's tik-tik
To the blowing wind
Which plays with my hair

In the whirlpool of activities
To the inner stillness
I am right here
In this very moment,

To the running clouds
To the melting snow
To the glittering glow,
I am here and one

With life
Within and outside
Everything is included,
In the very moment
I am here right now

45

It's a Cloudy Day

White clouds overhead
White snow under feet,
Hands in gloves still shivering with cold,
It's a cloudy day

Mud mixed with snow spread all the way
Minus is the temperature in the midday
Cold wind causes trees to sway
Yes, it's a cloudy day

Half of the world has started sweating
Here for the change of season, we do aspire
Summers seem to be a dream far away
Again, as it is a cloudy day

White mist turning dark
In the midst of the day, it's stark,
People walking huddled on the way
Yes, it's a cloudy day

Nature is as fresh as it has ever been
Birds flying can be seen
The cold has planned a longer stay
Hey, it's a cloudy day

46

Melting Snow

Melting snow is losing its glow,
Becoming muddy on the edges

Patches of earth
Started showing up
Layers of whiteness
Are decreasing

Carelessly scattered snow
Like casually thrown pearls
On the earth everywhere
Is mud stained with a lesser glow

The snow is receding fast

For a few days it may last

The magical spell that it casts

Of this season, it may be the last

Ego

Ego is big

Relations are fuss

All are there

If need be so

Otherwise people

Will just go

The way they like

If you don't meet the needs

You are negligible

It is just putting in efforts,

Have to tickle egos around

Otherwise, things are bound

To go sour

So why are we not clear?

Why make and be dear?

With false selves

48

Sunday Afternoon

It is sunny outside
Soon going to be four
I am sitting in the bed
Having closed the door

Sunlight falling on curtains
Which have been put on now
In the blankets in front of the blower
Here do I wait to take a shower

Snow is scattered all around
Outside the room
It will be minus degrees
Temperature here soon

I am all at ease
Doing things at a slow pace
Neither have I brushed my teeth
Nor have washed the face

Yeah soon Sunday
Will depart
A day full of ease
Will be apart

Having enjoyed it thoroughly,
I recline in bed
And enjoying each passing moment
It's wonderful to have this Sunday afternoon

49

Too Busy Living

Too busy living
No time for writing

A long list of works
Waiting for me
To-do lists or daily routines
Are piling up,

The diary, the books,
All are lying sideways
The guitar and lessons
Are there to learn and play,

Movies are waiting
For me to be free
Which otherwise I watch
In a day or two or three

The friends and people
To chit-chat with
I like to avoid
As I have myself to be with

The trees, the plants
Are more familiar
The birds and the animals
Even the pebbles are more attractive

One can spend hours being alone,
The striving to seek company is none
The more willingness to know myself
The more ignorant I am, I do know

Want to take in more
Of this stillness, this silence
So busy living at this time
For anything else, I have no time

Never knew anything in life
Nor do I even know myself
Nor even anything in actuality
Nothing do I know,

Nor do I know
If ever, will I know?
Anything ever
But I have been lucky

Lucky to have been born
Been here on this beautiful planet
Provided for every need
And am alive

It is the first time ever
I am busy living

50

Soil

The basis of human life
The life-sustaining element
The power of planet Earth
So, the love resides in you

A deep connection with soil,
All beings do share
Oblivious of sustainability
We hardly care

The womb of earth
All the buzzing beings
Are there and living
Due to this soil, which is giving,

In our ignorance, we call it dirt
From this very dirt comes all the things
Call it food, clothing, or any other thing
Because of this life-sustaining soil, we are living

With time we may recognise our
Inseparable relationship with this
Element, which even deepens
When finally we merge into it

After the beautiful death
Does spare us the game
That which stops one from seeing
Actual vision of who we are

51

What to Write I Don't Know

What to write

I don't know

Admiration for everything

Does here grow

The body I am surely thankful,

But I can't help but care less

Not internally yet

Outwardly doesn't matter much

The mind does grind
Every thought that flashes
Sometimes I do check
Otherwise, I let it go

Things carry on their own
Eating, sleeping, just living,
More alive in nature
I like life very much

First time I have
So much time for me
To waste to muse
Whenever needed to be put to use

Yeah, life is uncertain
This time it has been proven
A small virus became a threat
Very clearly, people realised that,

Still, old patterns exist
With little pipping into
Now and then
Otherwise, everything is going on

No, I am not afraid to cease

Not worried about time to increase

I am too busy soaking in

Living in whatever the moment is,

I am much happier

To be alive and here

All the regrets of not having or not living

Are a case bygone

I am so much in love,

With the life I do have

Let the activities be nil

But I have a life to fill

So, there is life

To fill each void

Imaginary and artificially created,

No moment to get jaded

Or even how can a person

Ever get distracted

From which is constantly there

It's all complete, beautiful, and grand

52

Dissolution

The snowflake that touches the core
Coming right from the clouds above
Landing on Earth, getting dissolved
Not suspicious, just fully eager to merge

With so much free intent
No need to preserve itself,
In full vigour, it throws fully
In the process of annihilation of self

For whose sake, no one knows,
Still, the flake has the dare
To completely obliterate
Without a single moment's delay

The moment it is formed
It is filled with joy,
Joy greater than life,
So hardly does it care to strife

In full bliss, it lets loose
The very strings of existence
Let itself fully soak in joy
The drop becomes joy itself

So letting loose of the control
Gave the valuable liberation
To enjoy to the highest possibility
It started, unmindful of self-destruction

And why not, by now it had realised
There was nothing to be mindful of,
Neither was there any self left
Nor was anything called destruction

The tiny flake had realised joyfully

The wisdom of ages

It just became the existence itself,

It was the supreme joy itself

It came down on the earth,

With such a grace

With such abandon, it touched the earth,

Even the Earth realised,

The flake was not different from earth,

It was just the earth,

This way spurting, swirling, squeaking

You march day and night

No one knows where to start from,

And where going thus dancing

You know you are already,

A symbol of completion

All the qualities one can imagine,

You are the bearer of them all in perfection

Being so complete a world in yourself

Leaving behind all the places you touch

Where are you headed to? Who can know?

What is it that makes you go?

You give life wherever you pass,

Providing to everything that is there

What is it that makes you go in?

Why don't you ever stay on?

Could anyone ever stop the flow?

To some destination, you must go,

Maybe yes, as you never stop,

Or maybe you live this way

Maybe you exist in flux,

It's just a big flow

Places are to be left behind,

And you have just to go and go

53

Tuffy

My definition of love,
You a bag of joy
As if love itself
Descended in your form

You are a walking love,
Your bite is quite innocent,
Your bark is the roaring affection
Your whining is beautiful

The way you greet

All these cute expressions

You are my bundle of joy

You are the best, my boy

You are always on

As if always stoned

Dripping love and joyous ecstasy

You are my heart's fantasy

The way you grew

Each day, somehow, new

You are love running around

The playfulness is ultimate and profound

Your wagging tail

It is life's trail

How any heart can fail

The overwhelming outpouring

Shower of love

My dear joyful babe

In each step of you

Life dances unbridled,

Dripping out the best

Whatsoever life has in it

Thanks my love doze

For being there pure love shot

For the joy, happiness, and sweetness

For making the love to come and dance,

On life's canvas

54

Until When

Until when will one be

Involved in the game,

Keep on repeating

Again, the same

Daily life is same

For ages it's so

If have come

For certain will go

Learning rules to live well
As if going to live forever
Burdened with rules
Missing to live

Though knowing, still oblivious
To something which is too obvious
How can one manage to overlook
The very basic fact

No Meaning

This is a consistent flux
Jingling of mixed flavours
A flow full all the time
Be mindful or forget; it is your choice

Circulate as many theories
Or philosophies as much as you want
Justify whatever you can
Do however you want

It's not even the speck of flux
Neither does this flux care
For any amount of change
Or turning the world upside down

Million books may be propounded
Beginning with countless explanations
One may figure out the cosmos
Hardly, it matters anyway

All the melodies, the jarring noises
Are one and same
The nonchalant doership and inertia
Come from the same place

The thinking tanks, the emotional tornadoes
Fatiguing activities day and night
The most rapid changes or the primitive silence
Are ultimately not a thing

The din and the silence are the same
Success and failure are one
Life and death are apart
The choice and imposition are for sure one

Duality and non-duality

Have nothing to do with reality

Every reality is individual and different

No parameter to measure what it is

The flux that life is

It just goes on

Hardly can it care to

Attach any meaning to anything

Nothing is more or less

Nothing is good or bad

Nothing true or false

No labelling, no meaning, no teaching

Neither was nor will be

Whatever is on and on

56

Love

Love with all its pain and misery

The hell it could be

Is worth having

It only teaches the extreme that it is

It will make you fly

And float as if in the sky

You may unknowingly feel shy

Can't stop smiling how hard you try

It can make you cry
Your eyes won't dry
Break you inside
Hurt your essence

It will devastate you
Humiliate and shame you
Kill you with toxicity
And a hell amount of perplexity

It surely does elevate you
Into your highest form
Make you your best self
Jolly and light as foam

Heaven and hell in one go
Pain and pleasure in one row
High and low hot and cold
Its brass of life and is gold

Touches life to the core
Stupidest things and wisest thoughts
Total waste and highest value
All containing ocean life does offer

It will make you
Shatter and shake
Bring your best self
And then the worst

Maker and breaker
Builder and shaker
The brightest and the darkest
The nearest and the farthest

Love is all-inclusive
It will make you experience
Both life and death
And it's still worth the pain
Many are without any gain

But at least you lived
Love, successful or failed
But ultimately you won
Greatest life lessons you learn
Had a lifetime of experience

57

Thank You

Thank you everyone
You are so loving
I love you so much
Thanks for making life beautiful

You all are there
Life is a beautiful bed of flowers
With different fragrances
And various colours

For the short span

I am here on the planet

Thanks for making this stay

Beautiful and fragrant with your presence

Profound

The chirping of birds
Was never this intense
Neither one had the time to hear
Nor were they that much free

Now they being free
Hopping from tree to tree
Singing to heart's content
Listening to only their voice

May be first time

In this life time

Their songs are unperturbed

Not hindered by any other sound

59

Covid

You came unwanted
Spreading all sorts of apprehension
Made people frightened
With your immense speed

You shut the people in
Stopped all activities
Lurking through windows
Frightened of the unknown

Unknown and stranger
You are for sure
The world is fighting
But fighting with the unknown

Name everyone knows
Little description too
But beyond it, nothing
Of you they know,

Fighting in dark
With very little knowledge
With less options
All people are left,

You crept in unnoticed
And reside inside humans
You grow rapidly like crazy
Killing the very body you're in

60

Dear Gallbladder

Dear Gallbladder, gone away
Without you, I have got to stay
An integral part of my body
And generally, of this life, buddy

I lost you to acute pain
To that stone which got struck
Right there and gave you much strain
This body lost its one part

A holistic mechanism
Has been invaded
Things will go on
Though you are no more

The journey towards the end
Has been fastened now
Though it was always there
But it's much more evident now

If gallbladder can
This body can go so
The whole struggle and striving
Have proven futile, though

61

When I Cease to Be

When I cease to be
What will remain of me?
This body this mind
This whirlpool of emotions

All the drama will cease to be

The whole existenceThe whole world around
Largely imaginary, though,
Everything will go, everything will go

Escaping

I have seen myself
Running away from me,
Even a second if I happened,
To be with me, I will run

Even running from the truth
That one day, I will leave,
This beautiful planet
Sooner or later, maybe

Whenever happened to be

Left in my company

I will run faster

To anything or everything

Not more than second,

Can I stay here

It seems to be scary

Void, empty, and anxious

And the only way out seems to flee

63

I am Mortal

I am mortal
Bound to die one day,
Each fleeting moment
Is reminder of the same

Every day something dies
And is replaced by something else
And still, we don't see any reason
To see our own mortality

People very near and dear
And far off and distant
They are leaving their bodies
Still we are asleep

Closed eyes can just avoid
But not stop or change
The ultimate reality that one day
We have to give way

64

Nothing of Mine

Nothing of mine is there

This struggle, this strife
That ego and all fuss,
Has come to this end
All this is nothing, in fact

Birth, leaving, and unlearning
Trying hard to grasp everything
And now realising futility
Or a kind of process

Through which I had to go

To realise that despite the struggle

Day and night, nothing can be changed

And now, after giving up this struggle

And accept and surrender

Whatever is there started

Realising that it is best

Nothing is absolute; everything is perfect

It has never been me

There was no struggle

The pain was self-created

The struggle was self-imposed

Even this body, which

Seems to be me and mine

Is not there forever

Nor is me

The doer is no more

So all the doings cease

Now only experiencer

Is left unto whom life

Does Dance as it likes

This I had been a sham
It was nothing
There never was a doer
Nothing ever existed

What you are going through
I do understand, though
Still can't do anything for
To make you easy though

Whatever happened was the worst
We have been quite cursed
The pain is unbearable
The grief is unshareable

For a second, if the mind comes
To the present moment
The other second memory
Takes it back to that pain

We are in it
Can't escape it
Have to feel it
Have to live it

No other way seems right

Neither screaming nor to shout

The heart is rendered apart

It has lost its essential part

The whole wisdom fails

Nothing ever consoles

The gloom is everywhere

Nothing actually seems clear

Covid 19

To have this in a lifetime
Which is beyond normal
Something unprecedented
Very strange phenomenon

Either giving a one-time experience
Or taking away life itself
Though innocently growing on
Yet ruthless in its way,
Kind of innocent killer

It has opened
Noble ways of thought
It has forced a new normal,
Of living and being

Seems to be strife
A widespread struggle
With wide spreading
Virus outside

Really tragic is the outcome,
Still, the question remains
Are we fighting this virus?

Just observe and see
Without being threatened
Observing minutely
With a holistic view

A matter of concern
For the well-being of humans
Surely they are doing the needful
Diligently, whichever way possible

All sorts of emotions
And reactions can be seen
Everyone is learning
Unique reaction as a being

Deepened emotions, whatever type
Heightened awareness whichever way
Restfulness and restlessness
An amalgamation of aliveness

The virus is giving in all,
Beneficial or ugly by our standards
A break and a breakthrough
Very lucky as a generation of people

Not essentially, it is an enemy,
To humanity, consciously
It has just found its existence,
And is determined to grow and last

This virus has imparted
The great lesson for living people
That nature gives to all
Impartially equal opportunity to grow

The survival of the fittest

The theory propounded,

Almost heard and read,

But only now does it make sense

When corona seems to be

Fitter than human beings,

More disciplined, more determined

More persistent than humanity at large

It's not the time to panic,

Nor is to put blame

Just to observe how

Changes can come anytime

66

Contrast

What a contrast

Can exist in a being,

For one minute, he is

On the mountain highest

For the other delving in depths

For one second

Planning to conquer the world,

The other second sulking in

One corner of a room

In a second, knowing everything,

Whatsoever is there

The other minute groping in the dark

Looking for its own meaning

And knowing very well doesn't know anything

One second action is everything

In another action does nothing

What is the right way to exist?

At least I don't claim to know

67

In Search of Guchhi (Morel Mushroom)

Today we wandered

In all the nooks of the jungle

Sliding and sweeping

In the search of Guchhi

As it rained yesterday

Hope ignited to install

The new hunt for this

Beautiful and treasured mushroom

It is Sunday and a little bit cold
A huge power cut since yesterday
No use sitting in the room
Let's find some mushrooms

We started as a party
Then all got split
With a guide a little naive
And maybe not very keen

Thus, the hunt started,
Going from one place to another,
From one hill to another top
At some spots fully engrossed
On others, just jump and hop

We went on for two hours or so,
With microscopic focus
And childlike hip-hop run
In between, dedicated to the mission
And, of course, in pure light-hearted fun

Tiptoed through the whole jungle

Praying for Guchhi to be visible

Looking with the keenest eye

Almost sweeping away the woods

Guchhi being the holy grail

It is the beloved treasure

With a very hopeful heart and elated thoughts

And the futile action bearing no fruit

We came back from the jungle

Still happy and giggling

If not with Gucchi in hand

With Guchhi's love intact in the heart

If I tell the real reason for the hunt

It was not even Gucchi in the first place

It was the magical touch of nature

And the magnetic pull of nature

Which my heart can never resist,

Guchhi or no Guchhi, I can

At the slightest excuse, I go to the jungle,

And be there as long as I can

As I feel a strong connection to this organism

68

The Little Birds

I can't see you
Of course though
Very well I can
Hear you around me

Near me, those tall trees,
And are the bushes small
Your tweets are echoing
Through all these living things

Blending with the singing sound
Of the flowing rivulet
Sun bright, shiny water,
A sweet composition of music

The melting snow nearby me
The grass is crawling out from the earth
The river overflowing with
Snow melt water
Even the view is much sweeter

White butterflies flying all around,
So are the bees
Like the one who landed
On my hand

Flowers are also blooming
On some bushes
Light pink flowers decorating
The otherwise naked bushes

One eagle and some crows,
Are flying in circles,
In the clear sunny sky
And two mynas walking nearby

69

Eternal Winter

The white hills

Trees with snow on top,

The cold is not decreasing

The chilly wind blowing

Thus, the recurrent snowfall

The temperature does fall

The trembling morning

The shivering evenings

The sun chased by clouds

It's own heat, it may not be proud

The frequent power cuts

The ever-worn jackets

The shrinking Animals

Hands and feet numb and chill

The ever-wet roads

With melting snow

The life which is quite slow

No activities, just survival mode

Eating, sleeping, working - nothing more

Confined to homes

Nowhere to roam

Struggle to keep yourself warm

Deprived of nature's charms

It is everlasting, perpetual, eternal winter

70

Essence

Your face is the mirror
Where I watch my essence
Your smile is the key
That unlocks my heart

Your picture lightens up the day
Like the sun, you shine all my way
The warmth of your presence
Unbridles my inner scape

The love, the cute innocence
Turbulent and incessant
Like a river finds its way,
To the object that is you

Like an island or a planet
You have become the place
Where I love to live in entirety
Excluding everything that is there

The days and years
The moments and periods,
Witnessing all aspects that could be,
Are the treasure trove
I possess of thee

The joy in the vein
The pain in the heart
The most cared for being
Or overlooked and neglected one

Because you are the sun
That brightens, that shines
That which burns and gets burnt,
In the different aspects of what we share
With all the dark and light sides

I may get distracted by different goals
You may get busy with different roles
Good times, bad ones, we have shared
Immense pleasure, deep pains
Somewhat essential, some in vain

That sharing and caring,
That loving and wanting,
That need to be understood,
Loved and cared for is something

Which has been there,
I always want from you the unconditional love,
I bet you want more of that similarity

Your essence is all my essence craves for

71

Beautiful Dream

I have this beautiful dream
There is a beautiful hut by the stream,
The birds do chirp, and deer do scream,
I have this beautiful dream

The cow does mow
In the green pasture,
The calf does play beside,
They enjoy the sunny side

The butterflies do hover,

Over the vegetable beds

The bees collect nectar

From the flower beds

The squirrels play in the yard,

On the coffee table

The horse enjoys himself beautifully,

In his stable

The fields are lush and green,

The fish are playing in the nearby stream,

The bees are gliding in their hives,

I walk on the mushy grass,

With soft and gentle strides

72

Falling Down the Stairs

Falling down the stairs,

Brought forth the thought, "Who cares?"

I was in intense pain,

By my own self, I remained

The pain which was unbearable,

I was with my body

Seeing and feeling the pain,

In its entirety

I felt and expressed

The love for my body

Who was injured

And still conjured

The strength to go on

All I needed was me

Who loved all aspects

Even the pain that it undergoes,

I sat with it and listened to it

And found myself even,

Loving this pain

Which generally is deemed as bad,

Something to avoid and to feel sad

The painkillers sat where I placed them

But I loved my brave body

To be there resiliently

Coming out of dark clouds of pain

Making peace with it slowly

Sharing an understanding beyond

The obvious roles they seem to play

73

Don't Define Me

With your limiting standard
Don't try to outshine me

This whole trajectory of yours
That you yourself construct
For you, it may be ultimate
But it doesn't confine me

If the actions are not opposing
My mind is enough to thwart
These shackles that you assume
To be ultimate for everyone

I may be one among you
But I am not one of you
Throw away the tainted glasses
They can't measure the entirety of me

I have this free mind
That can analyse and access
See through your conditioning
And marvel at your pettiness

A heart brimming with love
The love that knows no bounds
Such a beautiful heart
Rare anywhere to be found

That refuses to even see,
Your petty tricks and tips
How you try to manipulate
Serving hatred disguised as love

But this heart, even with yours,
Foolish oversmartness accepts you all
Knowing very well you don't qualify,
To be held in such high love

From far off, I can smell

The conditioned stale beliefs,

Dipped in the sauce of cleverness

Shown as love, care, and affection

Don't you think a person who smiles

Whenever you act clever

Do read your silly trick and is

Let the kids enjoy the game

I am no part nor party

To this stinky slimy

Ruthless, judgemental bickering of yours

You enjoy the kingdom of fools

The judgement you pass on,

If applied first to thyself

You will come to understand

Your own knavery and ruthlessness

So just don't define me,

Don't confine me

This hell of yours

Will further shine me

74

Looking Back

Looking back on all those years
The years were filled with some goals
And the lingering fears
What how and whether we will meet them here

What are we here for?
Only the survival that too the better one
If you have to have all the promised things
How are they going to enhance the being?

Looking back on all the years

That which are spent with some purpose

And when these purposes are already realized

 What difference they have created is not known

Looking back, when I see

Where I am and where I wanted to be

What all I wanted to have, and after having

Has it made all the difference that can be?

I have these goals that keep me going

And I know in full awareness that these have been

Picked up from the surroundings for what is supposed to be

And it keeps us geared up

75

Waters

Those lapping waters
Do call me to them
That serene peace I felt
The sense of core connection

The perennial sound by the shore
The rhythmic music that played on
Somewhere resonated with heartbeats
A vast stretched heart was both inside and outside

The majestic sea was my essence only

It was a magnanimous version

Of my perennial existence

Which seems primitive like time immemorial

There is evident a connection

Which I have with this ocean

I feel it within

Throbbing in every part of my being

I am this, this is me

I have lost track of when and how

I pulsate in the ocean

And it sways in me

The inseparable bond we share

For ages or beyond time

Two pieces of the same existence

Though seemingly separate,

Yet one soul, one breath, one essence

76

On Sridao Beach

This is a beautiful tree
I have sat down
The wind flowing from
The ocean in front of me

The waves hitting the shore
The cuckoo bird coos
The warm, silvery sand shines
Is soaked by rolling waves

The coconut plantation in a row
It is a pleasant view to be seen at the shore
The shade overhead of the tree
With broad green and red leaves

The vast ocean in front of me
Soaring and swinging
Roaring waves frolicking
Catching and chasing

The wide-open ocean
The incessant wind, the shore
The coconut trees, the silvery sand
This very moment here is life

77

The Sea

This vastness has in it the crux of life

The depth it contains has the wisdom of eternity

The tides soar high and low

Are indicative of life in its flow

When the waters come forward

Are bound to go backwards

With the highs in life, we create

An avenue for the lows

It keeps ceaselessly going on to and fro

The very way life treads through and through

The way the waves collide

Contains the age-old secret of life

So does the sea

The sea, which is serene and calm, seems almost stagnant for ages

It seems it has crossed all turbulent stages

It gives off the vibe of wise sages

Who, after the meditation of

Centuries have come to be the wisest

Tides are the pulses of life

That shows the grand sea

Which is still and repose on the surface

Has deep-rooted pristine life

That which keeps flowing through these tides

To go on in order to form the cycle of life

78

I Don't Know

I don't know anything
I don't know nothing
I don't know what to think
I don't know whether to think

I don't know what I want
I don't know what to want
But seen drifting the paths
That I pick on way
Or from people around

Though I like everything
Yet nothing seems to keep me
These deep urges come from where?
Or are these just taken from here?

Everything that I have pursued
Whichever I tried to include
Has with time fallen apart
Then again starting from the start

The repetition goes on and on
Though little slack may be
Still, it goes on and on
The trodden paths offer comfort

If I have to see the Truth,
In its entirety and nakedness
When frills need to go
Whatever is lift is skirt

If that is the trajectory of life
Why, then, comes the strife?
The fight for survival
And to thrive gives us strive

You being here always every time

Still, you seem to be the farthest thing

Still, habits, patterns, and needs win the race

How easily wisdom gets erased?

What to do, how to be

Still remains in oblivion

As the social being, it's okay

But being beyond is what matters

To the core inner being

No pretensions are needed

Work and intentions are needed

And sense of awareness has to grow

79

Disconnect

I have been feeling this
Deep down in my being
Can you feel the unfamiliarity?
In my soul is set this disconnect

Have been trying to drag
To nudge myself in this worldly manner
Towards the worldly goals
And playing these presumed roles

It seems there was this cord

Which was a deep-down bond

The habits and patterns are there

But the cord seems to be shattered

The core which was there alike

Seems have grown apart

It became dimmer day by day

And seems all in there is dark

Which used to be there

Even after all the superficial

Upheaval and discord

The deep-down fire was there

80

The Rain in June

This windy rain
The cold one
Has come after days and months
This beautiful, calming rain

It has been a long time coming
Every other evening, it was expected
As the wind, the clouds used to come
Bringing the hope that it will too come

The temperature had dropped

The heat is replaced by the cold breeze

The dark clouds contrasted with green trees

Are rain bathed fresh and beautiful

The perpetual thunder

The subsiding rain

The cool blowing wind

The swaying trees

All are filled with freshness

Even the burnt trees are healed

The bushes, the soil has rejuvenated

The plants in the flower pots are enjoying themselves

Done With

Done with the outward
Drama, show-off, the act
Let's go inside as the
Time for relaxation has come

The strife is over
Let's have fun
Done with impression
Aims and intention

Why keep postponing

Being as doing has

Been enough now is

The time to be at ease

82

The Fruit Tree

This tree, which one sows,

Engages him only

Very lovingly, bit by bit

One grows it until he himself is struck with it

First comes the desire

Creeping out from the brain

The imagination starts sowing the seeds

Followed by actions, the plant grows

The plant that one thought

Will have the ripe fruits only

Has all the aspects to itself

Twigs, branches, leaves, and sometimes thorns

Even if after much time

It starts bearing fruit

They take a full season to mature, but the desires don't have

That much of patience

The fruits of imagination

May not taste like the real ones,

As most of the time

They are bitterer

With a tinge of sweetness,

Now what is this

I only wanted delicious fruits,

But here, I have a plant

Full of thorns, twigs, and leaves

That bears fruit that too seasonally

And the fruits are not even
Near the quality of the ones,
I had in my imagination
And the care I have to bestow
To the plant to maintain

O my God, I never thought
I will be struck with such a plant
This is the worst plant ever
With little less of what I expected

Maybe some other plant
Will have the fruits
I want to have
I will grow another plant
Which bears fruit only

Though this will take
A full year or two
And many seasons too
Yet, it is something I must do

Isn't this the way
We go on from one thing
To another, the whole life of ours,
Finally to realise

That the fruits of imagination
Are in the realm of imagination only
Reality has its own subjectivity,
And is not bound to our whims

In our transaction in the world
We can try to co-create
Let that creation be bound
To have the touch of the other

Thus managing all things around us,
Throughout our lives,
We keep investing our lives
Into things that seem to be
Promising to fulfil our desires

But the fleeting desires
Love the chase
The nearer you go
The further they run

Keep running until the day
You may come to realise
I got to stop
And let them come to me

If they choose to come
They are welcome, but on my terms
If not I am already
Whole and complete even without
The fulfilment of them

When you come to peace,
With the desires, even if
They remain unfulfilled
With the *tease* in heart
They cause, yet you still accept them

Accept them for being a part
Of your life, even the pain
Is all they have brought
After all, they have taught

That dark and light

Pain and pleasure

Are all aspects of you only

And you accept everything

And let them be for what they are

Let them play enjoy

Let them grow and flourish

Just love them for what they are

83

Nothing Matters

All the pomp and show
All the glory and glow
All the pace and flow
Nothing matters at all

Too much talk
About what should
Or shouldn't be
And no action following

Is mere a wastage

Of one's precious time

Which, if utilised in,

The proper way in action

May yield results

Where you don't have

To speak only results

Will show the change

That is beautiful and liberating

Binding with absolute

And offering you the bliss

Which makes you be in heaven here

84

I can See Through

I can see through

The petty games you play

With every trivial event

Your inferiority complex weighs

To harm someone, confident

Is your compulsive

For an authentic person

You have a natural aversion

As inside emptiness

Is so heavy

The dirt inside

Is smelly and scabby

There are insecurities you live with

Day and night

In the gloom of your sad existence

Your search for light

Ends in the wrong way

Your cruelty tries to find ways

By targeting and humiliating people

Your wounded ego may find a sway

Your pain, hurt, and suffering

Gets challenged at the sight

Of a happy, authentic, and capable person

The instinct to break, to stoop, and destroy

Hijacks you as a complete being

Reminds you of your lack

Your utter poverty, inferiority

Which you never took time to heal

The game you play is,
The two edged sword
Every time you have an illusion
Of winning, you have already lost

Fallen deep into the pit
Of lack, inferiority, and suffering
The pain you try to inflict,
Will make your existence a mess

I just hope you can see
What a losing game you play
I wish God save your soul
And eliminate the pain you are in

85

The Respect I Showered

The respect I showered
The love I bestowed
All the care done
You deserved none

It wasn't you
Who was of value
It was about me
What I offered thee

I held you all dear
You faltered in your fear
But I gave you a place nearby
To my heart, knowing very well

You are not even close to
What I can accept in people
But I thought differences
Only make us individuals

I stepped into every role
As I assumed, we all have a common goal
What I could I must
I was the person you could trust

I did so much
Even overworked myself
Overlooked your insults
And your petty judgements

I never failed to see through
Your snobbish, stupid flaws
But I kept overlooking
Equating them to little straws

Silly, stupid, biased, and derogatory

Treatment you meted

Seeing through your cleverness

And hateful glances so heated

But enough of that now

As you all crossed all limits

You chose failing to see

The kindness humanity bestowed on thee

As your silly games

Were never deserving of care

You didn't deserve all acceptance

Only neglect is what needs to be shared

Now I take back all the goodness

Offered to you out of love

Which you replaced with

Insult, hatred, jealousy, and snub

So, bye, be in your filth

The mud you love so much

Play the cheap games you like

Only the thing is, I won't abide

I quit trying to forgive

You all like a nightmare

You were for my life

I take my power and give your disgust back

Abhianandan (The Brave Heart)

Salute to the bravery

To the indomitable courage

The unique expression of love

For thy motherland

Yeah, it was the call of duty

Which you performed so well

Not a job, something else

It needed much more than that

Much more than training
Even more than skill
A pride in heart
And high respect held in head

Utmost sobriety was the way
Accompanied with decent manners
A head clear and balanced
Heart incarnation of bravery

Radiating aura, pleasant presence
You did transcend the physical essence
An emblem for bravery
For patriotism and pride

With all heart felt
Respect, we offer Abhinandan (Greetings)
To a brave heart, Abhinandan
Jai Hind